THE NATURE KIDS GUIDE TO

WOLVES

DAVID ANDERSON

LP Media Inc. Publishing
Text copyright © 2026 by LP Media Inc.
All rights reserved.

For information address LP Media Inc. Publishing,
30012 Variolite St NW, Princeton MN 55371
www.lpmedia.org

Publication Data

Wolves
The Nature Kid's Guide to Wolves — First edition.

Summary: "Learn all about Wolves, the Nature Kid Way"
— Provided by publisher.

ISBN: 979-8-89818-126-0

[1. Wolves – Non-Fiction] I. Title.

Title: The Nature Kid's Guide to Wolves

CONTENTS

WILD WOODS

Wolves once lived across most of North America, Europe, and Asia. Now they live in only about 10 percent of their old home range.

Howl! A gray wolf stands in a snowy forest. Thick fur keeps it warm.

Wolves live in many kinds of places. Some make their homes in thick, dark forests. Others roam across open grasslands or rocky mountains.

Some wolves live where snow falls for many months. The air is cold and crisp. Their thick fur keeps them warm in icy winds.

Other wolves live in warmer spots. The land may have tall grass and gentle hills.

Wolves need big spaces to roam and hunt. A pack's home area can stretch for many miles. They mark their land with scent to warn other wolves away.

WOLF WORLD

Wolves can travel up to 30 miles in a single day while searching for food.

A wolf trots across a wide open plain. It searches for its pack.

Different types of wolves live all over the world.

Gray wolves roam through Canada, Alaska, Russia, and parts of Europe. Mexican wolves make their home in the sunny deserts of Arizona and New Mexico.

Red wolves live only in North Carolina.

You can travel north to find Arctic wolves in the frozen lands of Canada and Greenland. Or head to Africa to find Ethiopian wolves high in the mountains.

But no matter where they live, all wolves survive by working together in packs.

BIG BAD

Thump! A wolf's big paws hit the ground. This large hunter is on the move.

Wolves are the largest wild dogs in the world. They are much bigger than foxes or coyotes.

Most wolves weigh between 60 and 120 pounds. Males are usually larger than females and can weigh even more.

Wolves stand about 26 to 32 inches tall at the shoulder. Their bodies can be five to six feet long from nose to tail.

A wolf's paw is about the size of a grown person's hand. Big paws help in snow.

BUILT TOUGH

DID YOU KNOW?
A wolf's bite is twice as strong as a big dog's. They can crunch right through bones!

Snap! A wolf bites down hard. Strong jaws grip tight.

Wolves have bodies made for hunting. Their long legs help them run far without getting tired. Strong muscles give them power to chase prey.

A wolf's jaw is very strong. It can crush bones with ease. Their sharp teeth tear through meat quickly.

Wolves have deep chests that hold big lungs. This helps them breathe well when running. Thick, powerful necks add to their strength. Tough paw pads protect their feet on rough ground. Wolves can walk on rocks, ice, and hot sand.

SUPER
SNIFFERS

Sniff, sniff! A wolf smells the air. Its nose twitches.

Wolves have an amazing sense of smell. Their noses are about 100 times better than human noses. This lets them smell other animals from far away.

Wolves use scent to find food. They can detect prey more than a mile away.

Smell also helps wolves talk to each other. They leave scent marks on trees and rocks.

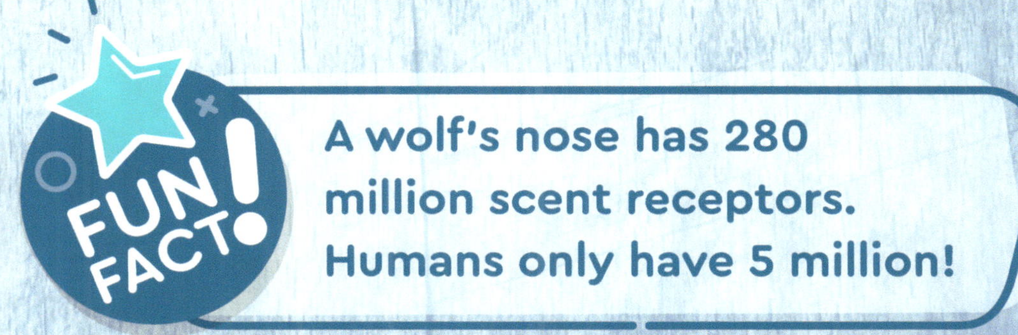

PACK POWER

Snarl! Wolves stand side by side. They face danger together.

Wolves are safer in groups. A pack can scare off enemies that one wolf cannot. They stand together and show their teeth to look fierce.

This teamwork protects them from bears and mountain lions. The whole pack watches out for each other.

Wolf pups stay at a den or safe place. Adult wolves guard the den while the pack hunts.

A wolf pack can have more than 15 members. The whole pack helps raise the pups.

MEAT
EATERS

Chomp! A wolf tears into its meal. Wolves love meat as their main food.

Wolves are **carnivores**. This means they eat meat. They hunt large animals like deer, elk, and moose.

A wolf can eat a lot at one time. It may gulp down 20 pounds of meat in one meal. Then it might not eat for several days.

Wolves also eat smaller animals. Rabbits, beavers, and mice are common **prey**. They sometimes catch fish in summer too.

They will eat almost any animal they can catch.

Wolves eat almost all of their prey, even bones!

17

CHASE DOWN

Wolves often test a herd before chasing. They look for weak or slow animals to target and attack.

Whoosh! A wolf pack races across the snow. They chase a deer.

Wolves hunt as a team. The pack works together to catch prey. They take turns chasing animals until the prey gets tired.

A chase can last for miles. Wolves can run fast, and they are built for long runs. This helps them keep going when other animals must stop.

The pack surrounds tired prey. Then strong wolves grab the animal and bring it down. The pack shares the food, with leaders eating first.

Wolves do not catch prey every time. Many hunts end with no food. So the pack must try again.

WATCH OUT

Screech! A wolf spots danger. Its ears stand up tall to listen.

Wolves are top **predators** with few natural enemies. Bears and mountain lions are the biggest threats. These animals may attack wolves that are alone or hurt.

Wolves must watch for danger all the time. They use their sharp eyes and ears. A wolf can spot movement from far away.

Wolves warn each other about threats. They bark, growl, and signal with their bodies. The pack responds fast when danger is near.

Wolves can hear sounds from up to ten miles away in open areas!

STAY SAFE

Rustle! A wolf hides in tall grass. It stays still and waits.

Wolves stay safe in many ways. They sleep in hidden spots. Thick bushes and rocky dens keep them out of sight.

Wolves are always alert. They watch and listen for danger. This helps them escape threats.

Young wolves learn safety rules. They stay close to adults. Pups stay at the **den** until they are strong enough to travel.

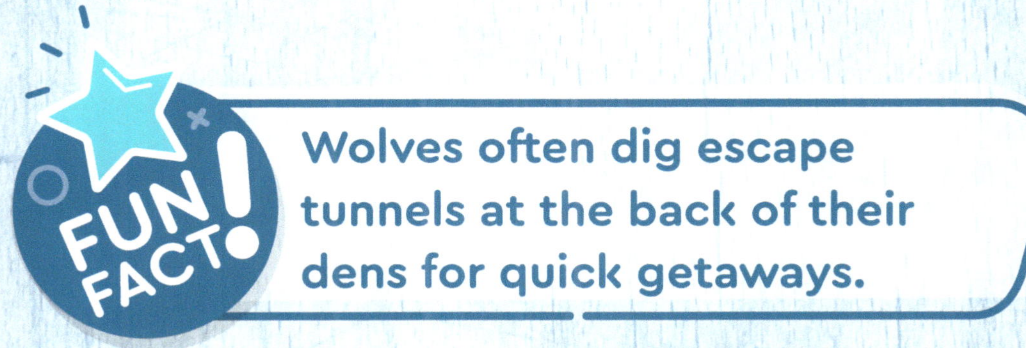

23

RUN WILD

Crunch! A wolf runs through the snowy forest, its legs moving fast.

Wolves are great runners. Their long legs help them cover ground quickly. A wolf can travel many miles in one day.

Wolves can track an animal for 10 miles or more. They follow the scent and keep chasing until their prey gets too tired to escape.

Wolves roam large areas to find food. Their strong muscles help them keep moving for hours.

Wolves can trot at about five miles per hour for many hours without getting tired.

DAY BY DAY

Rustle! A wolf walks on dry leaves in the morning light.

Wolves are most active at dawn and dusk. They rest during the hottest parts of the day, when cool air helps them stay comfortable.

Wolves spend time grooming their fur. They lick and nibble to stay clean. They also groom each other to bond.

Wolves love to play together too. They chase and wrestle. This helps them stay strong and close to their pack.

Wolves usually sleep for about eight to ten hours a day. They curl up to stay warm and save energy.

PACK LIFE

Sniff! Wolves gather together. They greet each other with wagging tails.

Wolves live in groups called packs. A pack is like a family. Most packs have parents and their pups.

Each wolf has a job. Some wolves lead. Others help watch the pups or find food.

Pack members care for each other. They share food and protect one another. Living together helps wolves survive.

Wolves howl to talk to pack members far away. Each wolf has its own special voice.

HOWLING HEARTS

Woof! Two wolves touch noses and stand close together.

Wolves usually mate once a year in late winter. Usually, only the lead male and female in a pack have pups.

Wolves howl to find each other. Their calls travel far through the woods. This howling helps wolves stay connected.

After mating, the female gets ready for pups. She finds a safe den. Then the whole pack helps care for the new family.

Wolf pairs often stay together for many years. Some stay paired for their whole lives.

PRECIOUS PUPS

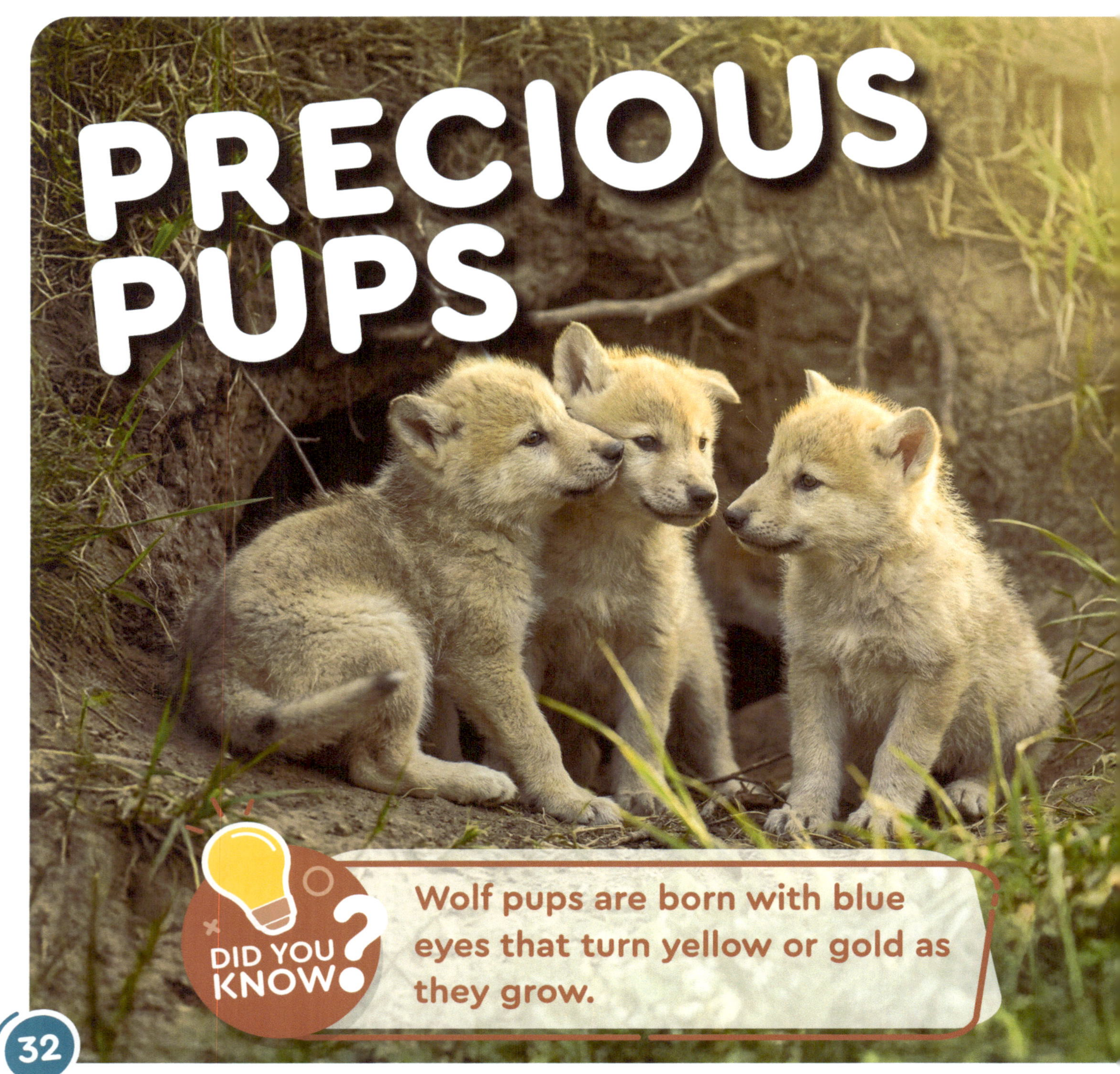

Squeak! Tiny wolf pups tumble and play outside their cozy den.

Wolf pups are born in spring. A mother wolf usually has four to six pups at a time. Newborn pups cannot see or hear.

Pups stay in the den for their first weeks. Their eyes open after about two weeks. They only drink milk when they are first born.

Pups start eating meat at around three weeks old. The whole pack helps feed the pups. Adult wolves bring back food for them.

By fall, pups can travel with the pack. They learn to hunt by watching adults.

RAISING PUPS

Yip! A mother wolf licks her pup's face. The tiny pup wiggles with joy.

Wolf parents work hard to raise their pups. The mother stays close to keep them warm and safe. She feeds them milk when they are tiny.

The father brings food to the den. He drops it near the entrance for the mother. This helps her stay with the pups.

Other pack members help too. Aunts and uncles play with the pups. They teach young wolves how to behave. Pups learn important skills from every adult in the pack.

Wolf pups practice hunting by pouncing on bugs and sticks.

SURVIVAL
EXPERTS

Howl! A wolf lifts its head to the sky. It's calling to it's pack.

Wolves are survivors. Ice ages, habitat loss, and hunting could not wipe them out.

Wolves adapt to change. When forests disappeared, they moved to new areas. When prey became **scarce**, they learned to hunt different animals.

Today, wolves are making a comeback. They are returning to places where they once disappeared. Their ability to adapt helps them survive.

A wolf's paw pads have rough skin that grips ice and snow, helping them run fast without slipping.

WATCHING WOLVES

Howl! A wolf calls out across the forest.

Seeing a wolf in the wild is very rare. They live far from people and hide well. Most people never spot one.

But you can still see wolves! Zoos and wildlife centers have wolves you can watch up close. Some places even let you hear them howl! These visits help you learn about wolves and why they need our protection.

If you are lucky enough to see a wild wolf, keep your distance. Stay quiet and watch from far away. Wild wolves need space to feel safe.

GLOSSARY

carnivores
Animals that eat only meat.

scarce
Hard to find or in short supply.

den
A safe, hidden home where animals rest and have babies.

predators
Animals that hunt and eat other animals.

prey
Animals that are hunted and eaten by other animals.